MW00511703

Expect the Best

Expect the Best

There's Always Hope On the Horizon

Katherine Robinson

Bardolf & Company Sarasota 2009

Published by Bardolf & Company

EXPECT THE BEST
THERE'S ALWAYS HOPE ON THE HORIZON

ISBN 978-0-9841745-1-5

Copyright © 2009 by Katherine Robinson
All rights reserved.

No part of this book may be used or reproduced in any manner whatsoever without written permission except in the case of brief quotations embodied in critical articles and reviews.

For information, address and editorial inquiries, please contact

Bardolf & Company
5430 Colewood Pl
Sarasota, FL 34232
tel. 941-232-0113

Library of Congress Cataloging-in-Publication Data
has been applied for.

FIRST EDITION

Cover and layout by Shaw Creative
www.shawcreativegroup.com

printed in the United States

To the glory of God

and
to all of my friends
who are
Acoustic Neuroma patients

CONTENTS

Introduction

Extraordinary events occur in the lives of ordinary people from time to time. Occasionally, they come in pairs to double your pleasure...or displeasure, as the case may be. Only in rare instances do they arrive in larger clusters. In my case it was a trifecta of a job ending, turning 50 and being diagnosed with a brain tumor all within one month. A person's natural tendency might be to jump off a cliff when confronted with any one of these! Fortunately, I live in Florida, a state so flat that leaping off a cliff is out of the question.

Ordinarily I am a glass-half-full kind of gal, but the triple whammy nearly overwhelmed me. The news was shocking enough by itself, but having to deal with the consequences proved even more of a challenge. I was out of my depth and my usual coping mechanisms failed to kick in. I did not know I had so many tears inside me, and I suffered many despairing hours wondering, "Why me, why now and what in the world am I going to do?" There were times when I felt so alone and frightened that all I could do was sit curled up in a ball in my silent house. I would nod off with tears streaming down my cheeks, only to wake up just a few hours later unable to go back to sleep. I guess stress and worry can do that to a person.

In time, I managed to regain my equilibrium, face these challenges head-on and, yes, even enjoy them…eventually. How I did that is the story of this book.

I suppose a story like mine is best told from the beginning rather than jumping in with the words "brain tumor," which are quite daunting in print and, believe me, even more so when a specialist says them to you out loud. So, let me take you back to 2008 and beyond and tell you what happened with my trifecta of extraordinary events and how I learned to celebrate them with the help of my family, my friends and my faith.

Katherine Robinson
Bradenton, Florida
December, 2009

P.S. I know! I know! A post script is not supposed to appear until the end, but in this case, P.S. stands for Personal Scripture. To help me get through my crisis I would find a particular verse from the Bible and claim it as my own. I even took the liberty to revise some words in order to personalize it just for me. Sometimes I repeated it over and over as a kind of mantra for the day or situation I was in. I *know* that the source of my strength came from the words of the Lord. I hope you find strength there too!

To that end I will close each chapter with one of my Personal Scriptures that was especially meaningful for me at the time.
So here it goes.

But the Lord stood with me and gave me strength so that I might preach the Good News in its entirety for all the Gentiles to hear. And he rescued me from certain death.
2 Timothy 4:17

Beginnings

Let me begin by telling you a bit about my background.

I was born and raised in Terre Haute, Indiana, as the oldest of three girls. My parents, Betty and Charlie Mattick, have been married for more than 50 years. Their love for each other has been an inspiration to me. My sisters, Beth Dailey and Charlene Seidner, are my best friends. We are a close family. While we may not all get together in person, we do speak with each other on a regular basis through e-mail, texting and phone calls.

Church was a large part of my life when I grew up. My Grandma and Grandpa Miller were very dear to me and they taught my sisters and me about faith from the time we were born. They often came by to pick us up and take us to church for some service or activity, and they were an important influence on my parents' strong faith in God as well. I became a Christian at age 12 when I was baptized by Floyd Miller at the Union Christian Church.

After high school, my sisters and I all began our employment at the same community bank in Terre Haute – the Indiana State Bank (ISB). Today, Beth is a vice president and branch manager at a different bank, while Charlene works for the U.S. Post Office. But for a short time, we all were bankers.

As the oldest, I guess I started the trend in 1977 when I applied for a teller position during my senior year at North Vigo High School. The hiring manager offered me the job, and I went for training every afternoon during that last semester. My banking career at ISB took me from bank teller to teller trainer, and I made some lifelong friends there.

In 1981, I joined the flock of snowbirds heading for Florida. When they returned up north for the summer, I decided to stay, and I have made my home in in the Sunshine State to this day.

Upon relocating to the Gulf Coast of Florida, I was hired by Barnett Bank, a well-respected company in the Florida banking community. Barnett gave me experience and training which allowed me to eventually move from the retail side to my favorite area of banking and business: the human resources department. After I left Barnett Bank – which was later sold to Bank of America – I served as a human resources leader for many years at several other banks. Over the course of my 30-year career, I have learned a great deal and met some amazing people.

During the mid-1980s, I found my soul mate. His name was Ralph and he was a police officer. We married after dating for a year. I loved him so much and signed cards I sent him ILYMTACLA, which stood for "I love you more than anyone could love anybody." We were a perfect match in so many ways. We took great trips together to exotic places like Barbados, Bonaire off the coast of Venezuela, Cozumel and Roatan in Honduras. We made plans that when I turned 50, I would quit working, as he would already be retired, and we would sail the seas together, delivering boats all over the Caribbean.

Unfortunately, the best-laid plans did not pan out. In 2004, after 19 years together, Ralph and I agreed to separate for good.

Right before the divorce became final, I decided to use my new-found freedom and extra time to go back to college. I had taken lots of courses through the years and taught many classes to bankers and others, but I had never finished my college degree. So, in the Fall of 2004 I registered at Eckerd College and threw myself into the life of a college student while working full time. It was the perfect thing for me and gave me a renewed sense of purpose. I re-discovered my love of learning and met some great new friends at Eckerd.

In the meantime, as the economic pendulum continued to swing upward in 2004 and 2005, a little community bank was formed in Bradenton, Florida. I joined Freedom Bank as the Human Resources Manager in early 2006 and continued to enjoy the upswing through the next year.

Freedom Bank had big growth plans. We were going to open several branches over the course of the next few years and, like many other community banks, we were looking forward to being bought out down the road by a bigger bank to give the shareholders a good return on their investment.

In May 2007, I graduated from Eckerd with distinction and high honors. I am proud to say that I was nominated by my peers and professors to give one of the commencement speeches, which was one of the most wonderful moments of my life.

Things were looking up for me all around.

The Lord will fulfill his purpose for me; your love, O Lord, endures forever – do not abandon the works of your hands.

Psalm 138:8

Running toward the Future

Looking back now, there were dark clouds of economic troubles gathering on the horizon starting in 2007 – I will talk about how they affected me personally later – but who knew at the time that our financial system would teeter on the brink of disaster with the failure of Lehman Brothers and the near collapse of AIG, Goldman Sachs and Bank of America? Who could foretell what a rocky roller coaster we'd be on? I certainly didn't.

Except for my 50th birthday in November, I expected 2008 to be an ordinary year. Well, there was the presidential election, which brings its own kind of excitement and national media attention. But while I'd be watching with fascination, I wouldn't let it affect my day-to-day life. For me, the year began with a focus on my health.

Physical health is something I always seem to be working on. I am either on a diet or some new exercise program. Early in 2008, I decided to go on a personal training regime with the goal of running a half marathon. I was determined to have my 50th year shape up to be a healthy one.

In 2007, my sister Beth had joined a local running club in Terre Haute. She started out slowly with a plan put together by a group of people that were expert runners, trained with them, and then ran the Indianapolis Half Marathon. The "Indy Mini," as we Hoosiers call it, is the nation's largest half marathon, boasting nearly 40,000 runners!

To support Beth, I went to my gym in Bradenton and got on one of the stationary bicycles and pedaled for 13.1 miles. Ouch! That hurt since I had not been training, but I don't regret it. I sent her good thoughts and prayers of strength and energy all morning. As I pedaled, I visualized her running around the Indianapolis Motor Speedway and then crossing the finish line. Beth completed the race, and I will never forget talking with her by phone afterwards. I don't know which of us was more excited!

So it wasn't hard for Beth to convince me that we had to run the next Indy Mini together with our younger sister, Charlene. At the time, it seemed like such a good idea that I set a goal for myself to run two half marathons! But when December came around and it was time to begin training, I admit to saying "ugh."

The physical goals that I set for 2008 seemed impossible to reach. Keep in mind that I had never run a road race before. Through the years, I had signed up for a one-mile fun run or some other such event, but even then I usually walked a good portion of the distance. As far as running, I am slow! In the story of the tortoise and the hare you can guess which one I am.

A half marathon is 13.1 miles, and most people don't just go out and run or walk that far. Fortunately, I had the help and wisdom of others with more experience than me. My good friends Tobi Martino and Rich "Rico" Hull provided invaluable support during this time. Rico, who has run many marathons, was delighted to set me up on a training schedule, and Tobi gave me a journal for Christmas. Both the schedule and the journal proved very useful.

Running a half marathon is not easy, though, and I do not want to minimize the importance of training and preparation. My personal fitness trainer, Mason, was an experienced runner, and she gave me a lot of tips to help me prepare for the Indy Mini in May 2008. She also suggested I sign up for a half marathon in Sarasota in February. With her coaching and support I not only registered, but I actually finished!

It was still dark when I made my way to the 7 a.m. starting line. The sunrise eventually illuminated our path through a beautiful part of the city right along Sarasota Bay, and as the day continued, we were greeted by hundreds of well-wishers ringing cow bells and encouraging us with claps and whistles. The water stops came along at just the right time and I had a blast for three hours. Well, mostly it was a blast. Around mile 8 my back started aching, and I kept asking myself, "Now why did I do this?" But you know, you just keep on going and never give up. By mile 12 I was dog-tired, but also elated because I knew I could do one more mile.

For all of you full marathon runners out there, I stand – or jog – in awe of you. Let me give you some perspective about how it was when I finished the race: I ran across the finish line for that half marathon behind the winner of the full marathon! (See, I told you I was the turtle in that story.) As I was nearing the finish line, a fast-paced runner came up behind me, followed closely by a police motorcycle. I knew this guy was about to finish 26.2 miles, so I kicked it up a notch and stayed close to him, cheering him and myself on as I ran.

Wow! That was something. I was so proud of him, and me, too. I met my goal of finishing in three hours: my final time was 2:58:32!

I must confess, though, that I nearly hyperventilated at the finish line because I was so ecstatic. A lot of friends who are runners had told me that when they finished their first half or full marathon, they were immediately overcome with emotion to the point where some of them cried like a baby. It is incredible with the crowds cheering you on, the music blaring, the announcers calling your name and finish time, and the volunteers right there to give you a medal and congratulate you. The knowledge that you have completed the race is truly an exhilarating feeling of accomplishment.

Later that spring, my sister Beth and I started together at the Indy Mini. Joining up with the nearly 40,000 racers is an inspiring experience. We both finished and rejoiced together at the finish line. If you have any inclination about running a full or half marathon, I strongly encourage you to go for it! I promise you that you will not regret it.

The boot camp classes, my times with a personal trainer and the half marathon training schedules all propelled me to meet the physical goals that I had set. And that was a good thing, because it got me ready to face the challenges in the later part of the year. Being in good physical shape is a great help during any kind of crisis!

Rely on the experts in your life! Seek them out. They will want to help you run your race and you need to let them. You will bless them by allowing them to help you, and then you will receive blessings through their expertise. Everyone wins! Remember: you do not have to be a world class athlete to do this. You do, however, need a strong group of encouragers and experts in your life that will help and guide you. I want to hear from you when you finish your first half or full marathon, and know this: I will be cheering you on and will toss the confetti in the air to celebrate you!

For the Lord God is a sun and shield; the Lord bestows favor and honor; no good thing does he withhold from those whose walk is blameless.

Psalm 84:11

Banking on Success

In early 2008, at the Freedom Bank annual shareholder's meeting, the bank's first president, Gerry Anthony, announced his retirement. I had chosen a seat in the back of the room, and I saw a number of employees wipe away tears as he read his farewell message. Many of them had worked with this beloved banker and friend, who had put so much effort into the creating and running of Freedom Bank. Some had been a part of the original team when the bank opened its doors in 2004. I could feel their sadness envelop me, and it followed me when I walked the corridors of the bank later that day and talked with other employees.

Then the new chief executive officer was introduced. His name was David Zuern, and he had the challenging task of leading the bank at a time when we had to find new investors. How appropriate and ironic that the founding president's name started with the beginning letter of the alphabet and our last CEO's name started with the last. The switch in leadership certainly marked the beginning of many changes: from now on things would be as different as A to Z.

Not that the writing hadn't been on the wall for some time; the market was changing as the real estate bubble burst and home sales came to a screeching halt. Many were caught holding a mortgage that would soon be much higher than the value of their property. Things had begun transitioning downward in 2007 to match the falling economy, and it was very hard to see how anything good could come out of the tough times that lay ahead.

By the summer of 2008, there were lots of closed door meetings. Rumors were spreading on the employees' grapevine that there would be layoffs, that our pay and benefits would be reduced, that the bank would be sold, that the bank would fail! I did not think it would get that bad, but this state of affairs went on for months and created terrible employee morale.

My 30-year career in banking had lulled me and others into a false sense of security for many years, when bankers and their shareholders had enjoyed consistent growth in stock values. I had taken the job at Freedom Bank, intending to stay until I was 60, contributing the maximum to my 401k plan, so that I could take an early retirement and enjoy my life and home on the Florida Gulf Coast. But the plan had to be revised as the prospect of change loomed on the horizon.

Just mentioning the word "change" frightens many people. I am fortunate in that I am not one of them. I normally enjoy the challenge and opportunities it brings. My attitude was: The sooner you can get your arms around the experience, the sooner you may enjoy the "change" roller coaster. Just buckle up and keep your hands in the car, and you'll be fine.

Maybe, though, like most people, I act much braver about being on the roller coaster *after* I have gotten off the ride. It's easy to say, "Hang in there and you'll be okay," but it is hard to believe those words when you are screaming and hurling down a sheer drop at a high speed with your body being whipped about. I would be lying to you if I claimed to really enjoy that part. It is the end result, the aftermath of change, that I like, not the process itself.

I hated the roller coaster ride that the bank was on during 2008. It was stressful for me and the other employees. Management was busy looking for ways to reduce expenses by freezing salaries, closing branches and cutting some positions. Overtime was eliminated from the budget, and the push was on to get deposits into our troubled bank and raise capital.

Things were also changing in the banking industry throughout the United States. America watched as the IndyMac Bank in California failed. Customers were coming into our bank and asking if their money was safe. The stock market began its record decline, and fear began to seep into our homes and our workplaces. About that time, "for sale" signs started to appear in many yards, and the word was spreading about a rise in foreclosures. It was a frightening time for local bankers, particularly the community banks that were struggling with non-performing loans and needed capital.

August and September were especially hectic for Freedom Bank. There were a lot of meetings and reports to attend to. From a human resources perspective, it became increasingly difficult to keep smiling and telling everyone that things would be fine, even for a positive thinker like me.

In August of 2008, First Priority Bank of Bradenton, one of our sister banks, was closed by state regulators, and the Federal Deposit Insurance Corporation (FDIC) took over as receiver in charge. By then Freedom Bank was operating under something called a Memorandum of Understanding (MOU) which, according to the FDIC's Risk Management Manual of Examination Policies, is an informal way of seeking corrective action. If these corrective actions were not properly addressed, then more formal administrative proceedings would follow.

It's analogous to a supervisor noticing that an employee has not been meeting agreed upon standards of performance, such as completing a weekly report in a timely manner and, after a talk fails to improve results, issuing a written warning. An MOU is like the written warning.

The follow-up step in disciplinary action from the FDIC is something called a Cease and Desist Order (C&D), which gives the financial institution a detailed list of things that *must* change. This is a very serious matter, and Freedom Bank received such an order on September 5, 2008. The senior leadership team met at least once a week to update the status of the items required by the C&D. At each one of these meetings our bank president, David Zuern, provided updates from the conference calls he had had with the regulators.

I admired that Mr. Zuern always held out hope for Freedom Bank. He was an amazing leader who never gave up making calls, meeting with investors and keeping the flag of hope flying for the employees. If you are a leader, I hope you never give up. When you do, your team will throw in the towel, too. When you have hope, your team will continue to fight.

After issuing the C&D in September, the FDIC immediately made arrangements for some of its representatives to be on site. I now believe that they came into our bank to begin the closing process, although neither the bank president, nor any of the FDIC regulators that showed up said so. But it makes logical sense that they would begin their preparation in the event that Freedom Bank failed.

When First Priority Bank was closed in August, it became an example to us at Freedom Bank. One of our employees had a son that was working there, so we had an opportunity to get a first-hand, behind-the-scenes look at how the process worked. We learned that the benefit plans were terminated, payroll came from a new source, all employees were put on hourly wages, and all references to the bank names in signage, brochures or business cards was destroyed.

One FDIC regulator assigned to Freedom Bank was one of the most professional women I have ever encountered in the workplace. I am not talking about her attire, but about the attitude she conveyed each and every day. Respectful of others, she would greet us politely every morning. Most of the time she worked diligently at her computer, and her interaction with bank employees was actually quite minimal, which was likely for a reason. Occasionally she would request reports or information from me, our IT manager or the CFO, and ask questions about organizational charts, floor plans, benefits and salaries. Her demeanor was always pleasant, never demanding.

One morning in early October, I asked her, "Suppose that Freedom Bank is ultimately closed in the next few weeks or months. If that were to happen, what is the best thing that I can do to be of help to my co-workers?"

She thought for a moment and then said, "Tell them that it is not the end of the world. That particular day will probably be one of the worse days of their life, but keep reminding them: It is not the end of the world."

That statement resonated with me, and it reminded me about something my mother had taught my sisters and me when we were children. She would often say to us, "Find something beautiful about today and keep that picture in your mind." Then she would add, "Later in the day, when things may not be going so well, look at the beautiful picture in your mind."

Remember that Jesus told his disciples that they would have trouble but to take heart, because He had come to overcome the world. Now that is a beautiful picture to keep in mind.

Faith is the substance of things hoped for and the evidence of things not seen."
Hebrews 11:1

Celebrate What?

In the meantime, my birthday was approaching quickly, and I could no longer avoid it.

People often plan to celebrate a milestone birthday like the half century mark with black for the balloons, as well as the plates and napkins. Considering the bleak situation at Freedom Bank, a dark color scheme would have been appropriate, but I couldn't understand why I should act as if I were in mourning about turning 50.

So on the outside, I kept up a good front, acting nonchalant about what it meant to me, but on the inside I was feeling depressed. At first, I really could not quite understand why I was so down about it. My 30th and 40th birthdays had been no problem, and I am generally not a depressed person, so I tried to give myself pep talks: Things were going to be okay in my life and at work. This was no big deal! People turn 50 all the time.

But the nagging feeling persisted, immune to my efforts to act as a cheerleader for myself.

It was my hairdresser, Darlene, who put her finger on what was going on. Aren't hairdressers some of the smartest people you know? They are usually great listeners and often have amazing insights. Darlene said she thought I was feeling down about this birthday because I was at a different place in my life than I thought I would be. Hmm? I think she was right. Life *was* different than I had planned.

I certainly hadn't figured on being alone. Just a few years back, when I was still married, I had looked forward to my 50th birthday to be my retirement party, too. Ralph and I would have our mortgage completely paid off and we would be ready to enjoy our time together as we prepared for the golden years.

As I recalled those "best-laid plans," I thought back on what had gone wrong. One Friday afternoon I had received a phone call at the office from a woman who informed me that she and my husband were in love and that they had been together for some time. I was so shocked I barely remember what I said to her. I know she said a lot to me because I took copious notes during our conversation, although I don't remember doing so. It was as if a different person than me took that call. I suppose most people would have hung up immediately, but somehow I switched into my human resources interviewing mode and asked her questions. We talked for almost 45 minutes.

I discovered that she worked as a secretary in an attorney's office. She and Ralph had met there – police officers often deal with lawyers over depositions and other legal matters. I found out that she had two young boys, her age, her telephone number and a host of other things. Although she would not tell me where she lived, I found out later for myself.

When I finally got off the phone, I did a really weird thing. I got up from my chair, shut my office door and lay face-down on the floor to pray. I choked out the words "Thank you, God" and begged Him, "Please give me the wisdom and strength to cope with this!"

I had just finished a women's Bible study at my church and remembered one of the recent lessons about giving thanks in all circumstances, including the involved discussion about how hard it would be to do so for something devastating. The news I had just received was a true test for that lesson, and I acted on it without thinking!

Immediately after praying, I did the normal thing and just lay there sobbing like a little girl. I was heart-broken. How could she have done this to me? Yes, I blamed her. I was very angry at my husband, too, but I was sure it was the fault of that woman!

Later that night when I confronted Ralph, he said that the affair was over and this was her way of getting back at him – through me. As you can imagine, the weekend was very difficult, filled with talks, explanations, tears, new promises, more talks and more tears. By Sunday evening I was so exhausted that I called in sick to work on Monday. And I wasn't lying – my heart was sick with grief. To this day when I read or hear stories of husbands who have cheated, my heart immediately goes out to the wife, children and other family members. It is likely that through no fault of their own, they are forced to deal with a terrible situation that often ends in divorce and more grief.

In our case, Ralph and I went to a marriage counselor and actually stayed together a few more years. We gradually rebuilt our relationship, and I was lulled into thinking that everything was great. As we started to plan our retirement years, I remember calling a "family meeting" one evening with us and the "kids" – our two cats, Sammy and Sophie. I was laughing and saying how much I was looking forward to our lives changing in the next few years and how great it would be, but Ralph seemed agitated and unwilling to share my excitement. I should have picked up on his mood about the future, but at the time I did not understand. Those words about our lives changing proved true, but not in the way I had hoped or imagined.

Things became all too clear when I discovered that there had been another woman. I felt doubly betrayed, by him and by myself. I questioned obsessively what I had or hadn't done to bring this on. I threw him and his belongings out of the house and sank into a deep depression. I did not answer telephone calls or e-mails. I tried to keep busy pouring page after page of my feelings of despair, anger and grief into my journal. But after the meetings with my attorney to go over what I needed to do to file for divorce, I would sit in the silent rooms of our dream house and cry buckets of tears and worry that I was now going to be alone.

Finally, I sought help at a place called Samaritan Counseling Services in Sarasota. My therapist began helping me grope my way back toward a new reality and future – not one that I had envisioned, but one that was yet to be planned.

I was 46 when Ralph and I got divorced and I ended up back on the singles track. I could not possibly think about quitting a job and sailing the seas now. I could not see much hope for the golden years. I imagined I would be working for many years to come and that my life would always be alone. Since I had acquiesced to Ralph's wishes, we did not have children, and it made me feel even lonelier. I selfishly gave no thought to my dear friends and family who would always be with me and let my sad thoughts take over the pity I was feeling for myself.

Some months before my 50th birthday, I sat and re-read parts of the journals from that depressing time – a mistake.

Reliving the pain and grief put me in a funk. It took my hairdresser to remind me that, although I was not where I thought I would be as a single person, I did have much to rejoice about. Darlene encouraged me to go ahead and have a party and celebrate where I was right then and where I would be in the future – wherever that may be!

I decided to follow her excellent recommendation and called my sister Beth, hoping she would want to come to the beach for that first weekend in November, when it's already cold in Indiana, and she said she would! We planned to have a fun dinner with friends and neighbors and, darn it, I was determined that my 50th birthday was going to be memorable.

And we know that in all things God works for the good of those who love Him, who have been called according to His purpose.

Romans 8:28

Happy Birthday

My birthday party was planned for Saturday, November 1, although my actual birthday is two days later. I knew that things were not looking good for Freedom Bank, but I really thought we would be okay until after the election. And, you never know! Maybe an investor would come forward and save the day! So, my sister flew into town on Wednesday. We were going to enjoy Friday night together handing out Halloween candy to the trick-or-treaters and then cook up some yummy things for a fun dinner celebration the following evening. It never got that far. Instead of a birthday party, I got a pity party.

On Friday, October 31, 2008, the bank president, David Zuern, met with the State and FDIC regulators to sign-off on the court order to officially close the bank. A press release was issued to announce to the world that Freedom Bank of Bradenton, Florida was being shut down by the Florida Office of Financial Regulation, and that the FDIC was named receiver.

In early 2009, a 60 Minutes special ran on television which offered a behind-the-scenes look at what the FDIC does after a bank fails. It was very well done and showed many of the details of what happens. There are a lot of people involved in the process, and everything must be handled with utmost care and confidentiality, including the use of code names and secure meeting sights to go over the last minute plans before the FDIC enters the failing financial institution.

But what no documentary can convey is the heart-wrenching feelings of those who have to hear that their workplace is gone. About 6:15 p.m. that evening the employees of Freedom Bank were read the official order issued by the court.

As had happened at First Priority Bank, every one of us became an hourly employee, to be paid by a new payroll company that would ultimately be reimbursed by the FDIC or the acquiring bank. We could no longer contribute to our 401k plan, and the process to terminate it along with all of our other benefits would begin that weekend. We were expected to work very late that night and over the weekend to close out all of the books and get things started for Fifth Third Bank, which had won the bid to acquire us, so that when we opened our doors for business on Monday, our customers would be greeted by their new bank.

There wasn't time to have even a brief pity party, because at least 50 people from the new bank and the FDIC came in as soon as the official order was read. FDIC employees quickly began to seek out the departments and areas of the bank which they were responsible for closing down. Other workers started to drape big black covers over all of our signs and began the process of throwing out stationary and other objects that carried our company logo as if to erase every single remnant and memory of Freedom Bank.

Meanwhile, reporters from the newspapers, radio and television milled about outside, waiting for any of us to leave, hoping we would share information for their stories. We had been told, however, to let the press officer from the FDIC or the new bank owner speak about the closing and transition process to the media.

I was amazed at the streamlined and organized way the FDIC representatives handled the transition process throughout the weekend. Sadly, they already had had a lot of practice with other bank closings. We were number 17 for 2008, and more would follow in the coming years.

It can take from six months to a year to finally close out all of the books and records and sell off the loans and other assets. One by one, employees are informed that they are no longer needed, or that *maybe* there is a job at the new bank. With the closing of Freedom Bank, however, for most employees the unemployment line seemed to be the final destination.

The officials from the FDIC that worked with the human resources department quickly found me and we began sorting through personnel files and getting them ready to be shipped out. Most of our computer access was still available at this time so I was able to share human resources files and information with them electronically. I was told that our medical insurance had been paid through December 31 and that everyone would get information about COBRA, an optional government plan that provides terminating employees with the opportunity to have health care insurance for up to 18 additional months without a lapse in coverage.

For me the weekend was a blur of paperwork and meetings with numerous people asking all kinds of questions. This was not at all how I had planned to spend my time. I did manage to call my sister, who was waiting for me at my house, to let her know what had happened. I told her that the birthday party was cancelled and that, frankly, I did not feel like celebrating anyway! Of course, she was welcome to stay for the weekend, but I would not be around much because there was a lot to do to close the bank. We were able to get her booked on an early flight back to Indiana the next morning.

It was a sad weekend for everyone at the bank. Admittedly, I took it pretty hard. But I didn't let anyone see that side of me. I excel at being a silent sufferer, and I continued to help close down my failed employer without letting on how I really felt. No Halloween or birthday celebration for me!

I know you must be thinking: Surely I was aware that the bank might be closed that weekend, so why did I go ahead and plan a party? Well, while I knew that Freedom Bank was in serious trouble, I never expected the government to close another bank right before the presidential election. I didn't think that either candidate would want any bad press before the historical November 2008 vote. But the bank did close and Freedom Bank was on CNN Headline News and my birthday party turned into a self pity party with me as the only attendee.

When I woke up on November 3, my actual birthday, I kept telling myself that it was no big deal – just another day. I was far too busy at the bank and simply *not* in the mood for any kind of party. I recall having to meet with some employees of the bank that Monday morning to give them the news that they were no longer needed and were now unemployed. I was still secretly sulking because my sister had left early, and I was not looking forward to the daunting task of working through the process of terminating everything that was associated with Freedom Bank.

So imagine my surprise when the FDIC representatives gathered around my office, brought out a cake and sang "Happy Birthday" to me. My amazement was genuine, and it gave me a tiny glimmer of joy. One of the FDIC crew went out to lunch with me, and then it was back to the task at hand. I have to say that the men and women from the FDIC that I worked with were wonderful and kind people. They took the time with all of us former Freedom Bank employees to help us through the difficult process of obtaining all the necessary reports and paperwork to close the bank, and they treated us with consideration and compassion throughout the difficult process.

If you are a banker, I hope you never have to go through this experience. But if you do, I promise you it is not the end of the world and I am certain you will find the FDIC employees to be some of the finest men and women with whom you will ever have to work.

Do I have any power to help myself, now that success has been driven from me?

Job 6:13

The Bright Spot

The first weeks in November, following the closing of Freedom Bank, were crazy. I had to get a lot of information shipped to the FDIC and to Fifth Third Bank, and meet with employees whose last day of work was coming up and counsel them about their options. It was about this time that I noticed a tingling sensation on the left side of my face. I figured it was due to stress, which can cause a lot of strange things to happen in our bodies. At least that is what I thought was going on. In any case, I was way too busy to make time to go the doctor to check out some silly stress-related tingling sensation!

I remember speaking with a good friend and complaining about the numbing sensation I was experiencing. When she asked me what I meant, I said, "Well, the left side of my face from my scalp to my chin sort of feels like I have been to the dentist and the Novocain has not quite worn off." She immediately insisted I go the doctor – pronto! – to get it checked out. I promised I would.

Of course I did not do anything about the tingling right away, but a few days later I called my Ear Nose and Throat (ENT) specialist and scheduled an appointment for later that week. By then, I was experiencing a weird taste sensation. It felt like I had a ball of aluminum foil in my mouth. Ick!

My doctor appointment was at the end of the day. I had been going to this ENT specialist for a couple of years now because of hearing loss that had started in my left ear a few years earlier. During the summer of 2006, when I experienced a strong bout of vertigo, I immediately contacted my family doctor and had some tests done. He referred me to an ENT doctor who diagnosed Temporomandibular Joint Dysfunction (TMJ). Apparently, I was a "grinder," someone who gnashes her teeth at night. The doctor prescribed a soft, low-salt diet and had me wear a night guard to prevent me from grinding my teeth. The vertigo never came back, but over the course of the next year, I lost most of the hearing in my left ear. A slight dizziness came and went, but I learned to adjust to that. Apparently, it was not the TMJ that was causing the hearing loss. After more appointments and consultations with another ENT specialist, it was determined that I had Meniere's Disease.

Meniere's Disease is a condition that affects the inner ear and causes episodes of vertigo, ringing in the ears (tinnitus), a feeling of fullness or pressure in the ear, and usually hearing loss in one ear. It is not fatal or contagious. I had all of the classic symptoms and my ENT doctor began treating me accordingly. Unfortunately, when the hearing loss was as great as mine, there are not many things that can be done, although the specialist continued to monitor my hearing. I learned to adjust to the hearing loss and the slight and intermittent dizziness. It was part of my life, and you learn to play the cards you are dealt.

When I told my ENT specialist that I imagined my symptoms were stress-related because of the bank closing and my

50th birthday, he was not so sure and wanted me to have a Magnetic Resonance Imaging (MRI) test done right away. It was now almost Thanksgiving and people were scheduling time off. I had things planned for the holiday myself, and I was procrastinating and complaining about how tough this was going to be to make time for yet another test and appointment. Oh well! I guess if it had to be done I would do it.

The MRI was scheduled right before Thanksgiving and I made a follow up appointment with my ENT doctor to go over the results on December 2.

As a side note, I would encourage everyone reading this to pay close attention to your body. Keep good medical records and be ever vigilant about your health. It is not likely that anyone else will be nearly as concerned about your health and well-being as you. Take good care of yourself! And when new symptoms appear, such as a tingling sensation or something else, do not wait! Get it checked out by a professional immediately. Get a second or third opinion and do your research. Our bodies are wonderful things and are designed to tell us what is going on. Mine was sending me powerful signals that something was terribly wrong.

I had never had an MRI before, and being someone that enjoys new experiences, I was actually looking forward to it. I had seen it done on the television show "Grey's Anatomy," and thought I knew what to expect.

On the appointed day, however, I had a terrible pain in my right knee. I could hardly bend my leg and had to limp into the office. Even as I am writing this, I am wincing as I recall how much it hurt. To this day, I have no idea what the problem was. It seemed that I was falling apart at the seams. Fortunately, that pain did eventually go away, but at the time I asked the MRI tech if she would take pictures of my knee, so my doctor could take a look at the joint. She said "No, we will only be focusing your head today."

I had shared with my dad about the pain in my knee. He told me that several people he knew, including one of his sisters, had recently experienced pain or trouble in their legs, so he added me to what he called his prayer "leg list."

My dad is one of the world's great prayer warriors. I talk to my parents quite regularly, and nearly every time he always asks me for the names of people that he can pray for. His prayer list must be a mile long! I hope you have a prayer warrior in your life. If you do, use that person. The Bible says to "pray without ceasing" and I know that my dad follows that rule.

So, if you are reading this and you have a special prayer request, just let me know and I will pass it along to Charlie Mattick – one of the world's great prayer warriors! In fact, I will join him in prayer for you. My dad does not have a cell phone, e-mail or a voice message machine, but he definitely knows the best way to communicate with God.

The MRI test went as scheduled. The tech injected gadolinium, an FDA-approved contrast agent, which looks clear as water and is non-radioactive, into one of my veins. Then she activated the mechanism that tranported me into the large donut. At the time, I was still trying to learn the music for my church's annual "Singing Christmas Tree" performance. So, I used the 45 minutes, along with all the loud banging sounds of the MRI machine, to keep the time with the music and sing all of the Christmas music to myself. It made the time pass and it helped me learn the words to my music.

When the MRI was done, I hobbled over to the technician who had administered my test. I asked her if it was possible for me to see the results on her computer screen. Some of my more sassy friends had suggested I do so to make sure I had a brain. When I explained this to her, she laughed and said, "No problem." I looked over her shoulder as she clicked through various screen shots. When one particular screen came up, I leaned over her shoulder and pointed to a bright spot on the screen and said, "Wow! Isn't that pretty?"

I am not sure what the technician thought when I uttered those words. You see, when an MRI is done with gadolinium, the test results will show the difference between normal and abnormal tissue, causing a trouble spot to become very bright. The bright area lit up like a Christmas tree was a tumor!

On the morning of December 2, I met with my ENT specialist to go over the results of my MRI. He came into the examination room and put the films up on the light box on the wall, so that we could look at the scans of my brain together. I got up from the chair, walked over and stood next to him as he pointed out the very bright spot that I had marveled at only days earlier.

All of sudden, though, I was hearing strange words – "Acoustic Neuroma" – and then "brain tumor" and "neurosurgeon." I suddenly felt dazed and dizzy, and the doctor suggested I sit down. I must have looked more than a little shaken. I know I felt that way. He said a lot of things to me that morning. Some of them registered with me and some of them did not. I wrote down a lot of things in a notebook I had brought with me to document our conversation, but today, I cannot even read the words I wrote because they look like scribbles. My hands would not stop shaking.

I vaguely remember hearing the specialist explaining that an Acoustic Neuroma is almost always benign and slow growing, so in all likelihood there was no hurry to do anything right away. He suggested that I take some time and look up the Acoustic Neuroma Association (ANA) and then he gave me the name of a neurosurgeon in Tampa.

I left his office like someone in a trance. I remember the front office clerk urging me to sit down for a minute, but I just wanted to get away from that place. It had pictures going through my mind of my brain with a tumor growing. I needed out! I needed air!

As I was getting in my car, I started to break down. I managed to find my cell phone and called my sister Beth. She knew I had been meeting with the ENT specialist that morning to go over the results of my MRI, and she had insisted that I call her as soon as I was finished with the appointment.

My precious sister took my call and heard me sobbing. I cried really hard. She had me repeat a lot of things because she had trouble understanding what I was saying – I was that upset. Somehow I made it home okay, but I can tell you that, if you ever find yourself so distraught that you are in tears, don't drive. Calm yourself down before you head out. And call someone who can be a voice of reason for you. In my case, it was my sister Beth.

But now trouble comes to you, and you are discouraged; it strikes you, and you are dismayed.

Job 4:5

Help Is on the Way!

When I made it home, I thanked Beth and told her I would be okay. Then I called Janet Cracchiola, a dear friend from church, who is married to our music director, Dan. Janet is a surgical nurse and she had wanted to hear from me as soon as I got the results of the MRI. When I said the words "Acoustic Neuroma," she responded, "I was afraid of that" – not really what I wanted to hear! She then told me about Dr. Jim Brandenburg, a retired neurosurgeon and member of our church, and urged me to call him.

I found the Brandenburg's number in our church directory and got Jim's wife, Nancy, on the phone. She not only listened to me crying and wrote down my name and number for her husband to call me later, but she also took time right then and there to pray with me on the phone. This was the first of many phone prayers that I received. Some days later when my mom and I talked about this, she shared with me that many people she had called about me had also prayed with her on the phone. What a blessing it is to be prayed over on the telephone!

If you ever receive a desperate phone call from friends or family members who are pouring their hearts out to you, make sure to listen and pray for them – right then and there on the phone. Phone prayers are so important, and easy to do, and the comfort that the recipient of your prayer will feel is indescribable.

When Dr. Brandenburg called back, he suggested that I bring my MRI films to our first "Singing Christmas Tree" performance on December 6, and he would take a look at them. I felt reassured that another expert, who had conducted research and taught at the University of Wisconsin for more than 30 years, would give me a second opinion. I can't help but smile now as I think back about him reviewing my MRI results in the quiet chapel area of the First Baptist Church in downtown Sarasota and confirming the diagnosis that I had an Acoustic Neuroma. Can you imagine looking at a picture of your brain tumor in front of a stained glass window at church?

In the meantime, though, after I spoke with Mrs. Brandenburg and my friend Janet, I actually did feel a tiny bit better. I dried my tears and decided that I needed to keep myself both physically and spiritually strong. So, after a quick lunch, I made a list of the prayer warriors in my life and the things I needed to do next. One thing I knew for sure – I wanted to do a bit more research before I called my mom and dad and told them that their eldest daughter might need brain surgery.

So I went on the internet and started looking. I also called the ANA which promised to mail out booklets to educate me about my brain tumor. I learned that Acoustic Neuromas (ANs) are indeed almost always benign and slow growing. That was the good news. They usually appear on the hearing and balance nerves within the inner ear – hence the "acoustic" in the name – but eventually grow in towards the brain. They can cause serious problems due to their size and location among vital structures. Mine was 2 cm in size – less than an inch – which meant it was medium to large. Because of the tingling sensation I experienced and the change in my sense of taste, my tumor was apparently attaching itself to the complex facial nerve (or seventh cranial nerve). This was definitely not good news.

Before fear and desperation got the better of me again, I managed to call the neurosurgeon in Tampa who my ENT doctor had recommended. I made an appointment for a few days later.

But then I did the same thing I had done years earlier when I received the phone call from the woman who was having an affair with my husband. I got down on the floor and I thanked God for the brain tumor. The Bible tells us to give thanks in all circumstances, and while this was perhaps one of the weirdest things to be thankful for, I did it anyway. Keep in mind I managed it only between sobs and tears and with my body curled up in the fetal position. But I did it.

As you know by now, my usual modus operandi is to deal with difficulties in my life on my own and to suffer in silence. I am a big, strong, independent woman and I can do it on my own! Well, I try anyway. The other side of that coin is feeling like a martyr, and I have to admit, I have relished that role from time to time. But not on this occasion.

After I pulled myself together again, I sent an e-mail to a group I call my "Highly Influential Friends" – a list of about 150 – and informed them that I needed to be immediately placed on everyone's prayer list. I explained that I had been diagnosed with a brain tumor and would probably need surgery. I told them to pray for my parents because they would be so worried, and I asked them to pray for all of the medical professionals that would take care of me. I requested wisdom for each decision I would make. And finally, I asked that God could somehow be glorified through all of this mess, although I could not imagine how all of this would happen!

Be sure to cultivate your Highly Influential Friends and keep track of them. You never know when you will have to call in the troops for prayer or help. Do not be afraid to ask for help. People want to help. Your friends and family love you very much. I promise that you will get the opportunity to help them in the future, but for now, recognize that you desperately need them. I am so glad I did not take my usual route of suffering in silence because there is no way I could have made it through December 2 and the days and weeks that followed without my friends and family.

I knew the call to my parents would be tough to make, and my sister Beth and I had discussed the best way to do it. So, rehearsing what I would say and with notes about the Acoustic Neuroma in front of me, I called my parents. I heard my mom catch her breath as I told her about my brain tumor. I emphasized and reitereated that it was benign, slow growing and didn't require immediate surgery. We talked for a while, and I asked her if she had any questions. She said "Not right now, but you will have to tell your dad yourself. I cannot talk right now and I need to think."

So, Dad and I spoke next. He listened carefully and asked some questions, which I answered to the best of my ability. I was trying to keep up a brave front. Of course, both my parents wanted me to come home immediately and move into the guest bedroom, so they could take care of me and protect me. I smiled at that and said that I really thought I needed to stay in

Sarasota for the time being. I had neurosurgeons to meet and to figure out the best course of treatment.

This telephone conversation with my folks was the first of what would become daily calls that I made to them after I got the news of my brain tumor. My cell phone bill shot through the roof as I logged nearly 4,000 minutes during the month of December. It did not matter because I *had* to communicate with my parents. I needed them, and they needed to hear from me – hear my voice and believe that I was okay.

Mom shared with me later that she and Dad prayed together after our call ended. She hardly slept that night because she kept thinking about what I had told her. Since I do not have children, I can't even begin to imagine how it must be to get bad news about your kids, even if they are 50 years old. My folks sounded brave on the phone with me every time we spoke, but I know they had some really tough times dealing with this situation, worrying about everything and feeling helpless to do anything about it 1,200 miles away. Their faith was really getting a workout!

That evening, I got a number of email messages and phone calls back from some of my Highly Influential Friends. I will never forget the one from my friend Diane and our subsequent conversation.

Diane and I have known each other since 1981. Both of our careers were in banking, and although we never worked at the same bank, we participated in the same ongoing education classes and other community events and became close friends. We have laughed and cried together over lots of things, both personal and job-related. Diane was on vacation when I sent out my call for help and did not see my message until the evening of December 2, so I did not get her phone call, but I retrieved her heartfelt voice message later.

When we actually spoke, she told me that when she read the words "Acoustic Neuroma," she could not call me fast enough. You see, her husband had had the very same thing about five years earlier. What are the odds that my dear friend would have two people close to her with the same kind of rare brain tumor? Her phone message was filled with concern and hope. I could hear her voice catch as she said to return the call as soon as possible because she had a lot of information for me.

Over the next few weeks I would learn from Diane, as well as from the Internet and various medical professionals, about possible complications and problems from surgery. The side effects could include injury to the cerebellum, meningitis, facial paralysis, hearing loss, persistent headaches, imbalance, dizziness and, oh, by the way, death. Since the left side of my face was already tingly and I was feeling a numbing sensation in my forehead, I feared that the damage on the facial nerve would become a serious problem.

I also would learn that there were other treatment options besides surgery available to me, including something called a gamma knife and radiation therapy. Every patient has a unique set of circumstances and a variety of things to consider. I found myself leaning toward the surgical route as the best choice for me.

Now that the news about the brain tumor was getting out, I wanted to be the one to tell my youngest sister, Charlene. She also lives in Terre Haute, near my parents, and is married to a great guy, Chris. Since Charlene is filled with compassion and has a tender heart, it would be difficult for her to hear the news, so I waited a couple of days before calling her. Bless her heart! She managed to talk for only a short time and had to pass the phone to her husband until she could get her emotions under control.

Charlene and I did talk again later that same evening and we both enjoyed a laugh when she told me, "Well, that explains what Mark meant when he said that it was too bad about your sister!" Mark Grayless is the preacher at Union Christian Church in Terre Haute, and Charlene had run into him at a grocery store just the day before. Because my mom had called every church in Terre Haute she could think of to get me on prayer lists everywhere, Mark was aware of my situation but didn't mention the words, "brain tumor." Charlene said she thought to herself at the time, "Well, how odd that he knows about her bank being closed and the FDIC!"

I am glad that I got to be the one to tell Charlene I had a tumor, and I love that I have such a sweet baby sister to worry and cry for me. Be thankful for the tenderhearted people in your life. They care very deeply for you.

So make sure you call on all the special people in your life. They really do care about you and want to help. We have a deep-seated need to be needed by others. And it really does feel good to help another human being. Think about it, by not allowing someone to help you, you are actually depriving them of a personal blessing. Ask for help and then receive it.

I lift up my eyes to the hills – where does my help come from?
                                    Psalm 121:1

Are You Wearing Your Cape Today?

The trip to meet the neurosurgeon at the University of Florida (USF) Medical Center in Tampa was both stressful and hilarious, although I can assure you, at the time it did not seem funny at all. The stress due to my health situation was compounded by trying to figure out exactly where I was supposed to go. Finding the medical center was the first challenge. Good grief! The directions were all but impossible to follow, and the office where I was to meet the doctor was in a completely different location than what we had been told by the guard at the gate when we checked in.

My friend LaVerne had offered to come along with me, and I am so glad she did. I wanted to have another set of eyes and ears in the room as I asked my questions of the neurosurgeon. In the meantime, she helped me navigate, or I would have turned around and headed back home in frustration long before ever getting there. We got lost and went to two wrong places before we finally arrived at the right office!

After checking in and filling out mounds of paperwork, we were sent to another waiting area. Hours later – or so it seemed at the time – a nurse came out and called my name. By then, I admit, I was not my usual pleasant self. When the nurse showed us into yet another waiting area and asked me to get on a scale, I had a hissy fit.

"What in the world do you need to get my weight for?" I nearly yelled at the poor girl. "I am here for a consultation and I am not going to get on a scale. I would appreciate it if you could just let the doctor know that I am here for this consultation - which *was* to happen about a half hour ago."

The nurse did not take my weight, but tried to explain to me that it was standard operating procedure.

I was not going to be humored. "You can weigh me if I choose to come here for treatment for my brain tumor!" I growled.

LaVerne was trying to calm me down all the while laughing at the absurdity of the situation.

Finally the neurosurgeon arrived. I had filled two pages of questions and, to his credit, he took his time to answer everything I asked. I found out enough about the Gamma Knife Procedure to reject that option once and for all. As for surgery, if I decided I wanted him to do the procedure, it would happen at Tampa General Hospital. He gave me his e-mail and phone number and said that if I needed to know about anything else, all I had to do was call or write.

As LaVerne and I drove back to Bradenton that afternoon I told her that I did not feel great about the USF medical facility. The doctor seemed pleasant enough, but the location did not feel right for me.

When I got back home, at the suggestion of my friend Diane, I phoned the Silverstein Institute in Sarasota. I explained that I had just been diagnosed with an Acoustic Neuroma and wondered if there was someone I could talk to about it. The receptionist set me up for an appointment for the next day with Dr. Jack Wazen.

The following afternoon I checked in at the registration desk at the Silverstein Institute. A feeling of calm come over me. The place had been easy to find, despite a traffic accident on US 41 that made me 15 minutes late. Fortunately, no one asked to check my weight before the consultation. Dr. Wazen's nurse practitioner, Julie Daugherty, came into the examination room and took my file. She complimented me on being quite the historian – I had documented my medical timeline and had everything color coordinated in a binder with dividers. She and I talked for a while and she told me that the doctor who would see me was one of the finest men she had ever worked with. I would soon find out why.

When Dr. Jack Wazen arrived, he took my hand, looked into my eyes and said "Now, how may I help you, Miss Kathy Robinson?" I was his last appointment for the day, and he spent almost an hour with me, answering all of my questions in a practical, yet kind manner. When he stepped out for a moment to get something for my chart, I wrote in big bold letters across the top of my notes page, "I WOULD FEEL VERY SAFE WITH THIS MAN." I made the decision right then and there that Dr. Wazen would be my surgeon. His credentials were impeccable. He and the other staff at the Silverstein Institute made me feel comfortable, cared for and confident that they would do everything in their power to help me. Dr. Wazen told me that he generally did this type of surgery with a local neurosurgeon, Dr. Ryan Glasser. Dr. Wazen's surgical coordinator would set up an appointment for me for a consultation with him.

That was the next hurdle I had to overcome. It was now December 9, and the earliest I could get in to see Dr. Glasser for a first time consult was not until December 21. Even though I knew I didn't have to rush things, I had now decided that I wanted the tumor removed before the end of the year.

There were two important reasons I felt more urgency than before. The first was health related. While the tumor was slow growing, the tingling in my face seemed to be getting worse, and I had lost most of my sense of taste. Second, my health insurance plan was terminating on December 31, 2008.

Remember, when Freedom Bank failed, all employee benefits were terminated right away, although the health insurance premiums had been paid through the end of the year. While I had the option of going on a COBRA plan offered through the FDIC, it had a deductible of $5,000. As it happened, I had already met my insurance deductible for 2008 and, therefore, a significant amount, maybe all of the surgery would be covered under the current plan. But I would have to have the surgery before the end of the year.

So on December 10, I sent another call for help via e-mail to my Highly Influential Friends. I told them I had met a surgeon I liked and trusted at the Silverstein Institute in Sarasota. I explained that Dr. Wazen to liked team up with a neurosurgeon for the removal of Acoustic Neuromas. So, in these last 21 days of 2008, there was much to do! I had to meet with the neurosurgeon, Dr. Glassser, for a consultation. Then his office needed to coordinate with Dr. Wazen and a lot of other people to schedule me for brain surgery. Operating rooms needed to be reserved and audiologists scheduled for the team. I had to remain healthy and make it through everything – all before December 31, 2008.

Unfortunately, as I soon discovered, a lot of people want to get medical treatments done in December for insurance purposes and other reasons. And don't forget, there is the matter of a couple of holidays in the middle of all that. I could not imagine how it would be possible to coordinate the schedule of an entire surgical team in that time frame. It would take nothing less than a miracle.

On the morning of December 12, I was in my office at the bank trying to get through to the neurosurgeon's office once again to get the appointment moved to an earlier date, and having no luck. After calling my surgical coordinator and leaving a tearful message asking if they could do anything, I phoned a friend who is in the medical field. When I asked him if he had any suggestions, he said I was doing all the right things. But all I knew was that time was running out.

I remember hanging up the phone and putting my head down on my desk in despair and feeling very sorry for myself. There was a knock on my door. I wiped my eyes and answered with a muffled "Yes." It was Larry, our IT manager, and he needed some information from me. He opened the door and stepped into my office. He never did say what he needed, but came over, gave me a hug and told me that "it will be okay." Although I did not believe him, the simple human contact and act of kindness made me feel better.

A couple of days later I phoned Pastor Bill, the senior pastor at First Baptist Church in Sarasota, to see if he could help.

I told him, "I want the tumor out!" and explained that the insurance deadline was fast approaching, but I had not yet been able to get the consultation appointment with a neurosurgeon in Sarasota moved up. I felt that I *must* have the surgery before the year's end and knew that there were *only* 17 days remaining in 2008. How could everything come together when *nothing* seemed to be happening? I was literally sobbing on the phone.

Pastor Bill listened to me, prayed for me, listened some more and then asked me a strange question, "Are you wearing your cape today?"

I stopped sniffling and said, "What do you mean? I don't understand your question. No, I am not wearing a cape today."

And, my wonderful pastor said, "Well, you are not super woman, and if you were not having a few breakdowns during this time, I would wonder: What is the problem with her?"

In other words, I had permission to cry and be upset. However, I needed to remember to turn it over to God and for all those Highly Influential Friends to stand in the gap for me. When Pastor Bill prayed with me on the phone and took the time to talk with me, I did seem to feel a little better. Jesus said in Matthew 11:28, "Come to me, all of you who are weary and carry heavy burdens, and I will give you rest." I needed the reminder that I did not have to go through this on my own. I was not alone. There were friends and family who would help me, and I needed to stop acting like the Lone Ranger.

So, I got off of the phone, took a deep breath and tried to focus on something else. It was time to send out another e-mail to my Highly Influential Friends and ask them to pray for a miracle in the form of an earlier appointment with Dr. Glasser.

I thanked them in advance for their prayers and ended my e-mail with, "Expect it to happen!"

And you know what? When I wrote those words, I think, deep inside, I did begin to expect it to happen.

On the morning of December 15, the neurosurgeon's office phoned to tell me that they could get me in the next day! So after sharing the good news with my Highly Influential Friends, I asked them to pray that Dr. Glasser and Dr. Wazen would be able to coordinate schedules to get their team ready for my brain surgery, all within the next 16 days. I ended the e-mail message with the words, "Stay tuned…next e-mail WILL have that surgery date BEFORE 12/31/08."

I love that I had the faith to write those words on December 15. I am thankful that the Lord enveloped me with a sense of peace about the situation. I can hardly wait to tell you what happened next!

When I met with Dr. Glasser on the morning of December 16, I was surprised at his youthful appearance. He was engaging and attentive as we spoke together. He took a look at my MRI films and asked me some questions. I filled out more forms and paperwork. I told him about my bank failing and the insurance problem. When I pleaded with him that if there were any way possible he could help get the surgery scheduled by the end of the year, he smiled and said that he and Dr. Wazen had just coordinated their schedules along with all the other people that would need to be there. He hoped I would be okay with a surgery date of December 30. Can you imagine how I felt? More tears, but this time, I assure you, they were tears of joy.

So that afternoon, I wrote my Highly Influential Friends the good news that our prayers had been answered. I told them that the Great Physician along with Drs. Wazen and Glasser would be taking good care of me, and I invited everyone to Sarasota Memorial Hospital for New Years Eve. My Acoustic Neuroma would be coming out the day before, on December 30, and I would be starting 2009 tumor-free. I told my friends that although the surgery would take seven hours or so, followed by a day in ICU, I was planning a swift recovery and a big party!

Seek the Kingdom of God above all else, and live righteously, and he will give you everything you need.
                              Matthew 6:33

Medicated and Motivated with Frosty Pink Lip Gloss

For nearly 10 years I have been a part of the annual Singing Christmas Tree at the First Baptist Church in downtown Sarasota. There are usually about 100 or more choir members standing shoulder to shoulder on a nearly 30-foot steel frame scaffolding covered with greenery and more than 10,000 twinkle lights. Accompanied by a talented orchestra, we sing 10 or 12 songs interspersed with scenes that tell the Christmas story. Sometimes there are flying angels gliding across the sanctuary, and we almost always have a real baby playing the part of the baby Jesus. We rehearse starting in September and perform the show nine or 10 times over the course of the first two weekends in December to sold out crowds.

I always say I am joyfully exhausted when the last performance is over, and every year end up with what I call my "tree" cold. As you can imagine, with all of those people in the audience and all of us standing in the tree, combined with a hectic time of year, it's not surprising that I'd end up with a cold.

What was a surprise, though, was that I did not catch my annual "tree" cold in 2008. Keep in mind that it was vitally important that I remain healthy during this time, and although I could have stayed away from the church, I decided to go ahead and join in the festivities. I knew that it would be good to have this joy be part of me at this difficult time!

With the the surgery date settled, it was now time to make plans. Knowing I had only a little time before the December 30 appointment definitely had me motivated to get things in order at my home and make the place ready for the people that would be staying with me and coming by to help. I was planning on a swift recovery, though, and did not see much need for all the fuss. Some people insisted I prepare to be out of commission for at least two weeks, so I made plans to be away from work at least that long.

Knowing that I would be in the hospital for several days, I also wanted to have fun – well, as much fun as a person undergoing brain surgery can have. I had never stayed in the hospital before, except when I was born, and I certainly do not remember that. In any case, since I was certain I would be there for New Years Eve, I needed to make sure that I had party hats, champagne, noise makers and confetti. And in one of the messages to my Highly Influential Friends I told everyone to make sure I had on my frosty pink lip gloss. I do not know what it is about lip gloss. I may not fuss with my hair or make-up, but you can bet I have the lip gloss on, even if it is for a trip to the grocery store, a workout at the gym or running out to the mailbox. Somehow it just makes me feel better.

I was glad that my sister Beth would be in the waiting room while I had my surgery and stay with me afterwards. My parents wanted to come, too, but I encouraged them to stay at home in Indiana. I reminded them that Beth would keep them updated throughout the day of my surgery and in the days following as I recovered. I knew I would have worried about them being in a strange place and well out of their comfort zone. Since they were going to be worried about me anyway, I figured it might as well be in familiar surroundings.

Beth's flight arrived on December 29, surgery eve, at the Sarasota-Bradenton airport about 11:00 p.m. So we went out to an all-night Perkins restaurant for my "last supper" of 2008. After midnight, I could have no more water or food, so we treated ourselves to eggs and pancakes. We were both giddy and laughing so hard at the silliest things that tears came to my eyes, but it felt good.

Beth suffered through my description of all of the things I had planned for her to do. I had put together a list of about 60 people for her to call with the expected good news following the surgery. I gave her my living will, a list of my bank accounts, keys to the house and my car, a map of Sarasota and a "what if" list. I had put them all into an attaché case with color coded envelopes and alphabetized files. To say I had been just a bit compulsive would have been an understatement. Beth just rolled her eyes at me.

Most of my "what if" list was serious, but some of the items were quite silly:

- If I do not have lip-gloss on when you come to visit, please apply it often. You will find it in the Kathy-supply kit.
- If I have something hanging out of my nose, please remove it.

- If I start snoring, please shake me until I quit.
- If I start saying strange things, sort of punch me until I stop talking! I'll probably be on morphine, so it won't hurt much, however hard you punch. This is your chance to make up for all those times I gave you stitches when we were growing up.
- If the room suddenly becomes stinky, spritz some cologne around – it will be in your Kathy-supply kit.

The final "what if" was for Beth: "If I forget to tell you how blessed I am to have a sister like you to be here with me – look in the mirror and know that I love that person very much and that I am very grateful that you are 'my person'!"

Although we did not go to sleep until after 1:30 a.m., we both were able to rest for a few hours. My surgical instructions stated that I was to take two showers before I arrived at the hospital at 5:30 a.m., so I got up in plenty of time for a double scrub-a-dub-dub.

When we arrived at Sarasota Memorial Hospital for check-in, I was determined to be brave, so I laughed and kidded around with Beth. At the front desk we received instructions to go to Elevator D and take it to the 4th floor. There, I had to sign in and give my name and information once again. We didn't have to wait long before a nurse came and showed us to a small curtained-off area that offered a little privacy from all the other patients who were there to have surgery that day as well. I quickly changed into a hospital gown and got into the bed.

When I looked up I saw my pastor and his wife along with Barbara and Dave Kiracofe, another couple from my church, walking toward us. Can you imagine? It was barely 6:00 a.m. and they had come to see me! I introduced them to my sister and we all chatted for a bit.

Around 6:30 a.m., the two members of the audiologist team arrived to check on me and to take preliminary readings on my facial nerves. They hooked me up to all kinds of tiny electrodes and took notes. Then both of them took my hands, looked me in the eye and said they would be in the operating room the whole time, monitoring my progress. They promised they would take good care of me, and I believed them.

At the suggestion of my pastor, we all took each other's hands while he gave a heartfelt prayer for healing and blessings. I was almost done with my list of things to do, so with nothing else to check off, I started to feel a bit teary-eyed.

The anesthesiologist came in, introduced himself to me and made some notes in his folder. Everyone that greeted me in the hospital always asked me my name and birth date first and then confirmed the type of surgery and the side of my head where the tumor was located. The anesthesiologist promised to be back shortly.

Then my neurosurgeon, Dr. Glasser, popped in for a quick hello and to ask me how I was doing. He took a look at some charts and then assured me that he and Dr. Wazen would take very good care of me. With that, he turned around and walked out to prepare for my seven-hour surgery.

Gulp! Now it was time to start getting nervous. All the research I had done about possible complications from surgery came back to me. I would, in all likelihood, completely lose the hearing in my left ear. I could have more pronounced problems with tinnitus, dizziness and balance. And one side of my face could be permanently paralyzed. But what scared me most of all was the possibility of getting a cerebrospinal fluid leak (CSF), in which the fluid surrounding my brain would be seeping out through the incision the surgeons made, with the added danger of contracting meningitis. I would have to be very careful after surgery not to sneeze or blow my nose hard. How in the world could I keep from sneezing?

I had been so brave and upbeat until then, but all of these thoughts were racing through my mind. I looked at my sister and started to cry. Beth came over to hug me and said, "You are going to be fine."

My voice caught as I told her, "I know, I know I will – but I am scared!" It was about this time that the anesthesiologist joined us again, took a look at me and said "Time for her to go to sleep! Say good night, Kathy!"

As he injected the fluid into my vein, I did not even get the words "good night" out. Rats! And I had wanted to see what the operating room looked like and check out the scenery in there, but I was out for the night, or rather the day. I find it so amazing that one moment you are alert, awake and laughing (or crying) and then – snap – you are out as if someone just switched off the light. Then someone shaves your hair and someone else drills a hole in your head to take a brain tumor out. How does that happen? The worlds of science and medicine astound me! God bless everyone in those fields!

It was 7:30 a.m. Beth was now on her own, although later she told me that my church friends invited her to breakfast. She thanked them and tearfully explained that she needed some time to herself right then. Bless her heart! She then went downstairs to get a breath of fresh air. It was a beautiful late December day. She was near the emotional breaking point herself and needed to be calmed down. She phoned her husband, Mark, and he heard the fear in her voice. So he talked to her to get her mind off what was happening to me. When she had pulled herself together, she phoned our parents and began giving them the first of many reports.

Several times that day the surgeons would send someone to update her on my progress. Each time they informed her that everything was going great. My friend LaVerne came by the hospital and went to lunch with her. Then Beth returned to the waiting room to, well, wait. It was nearly 3:00 that afternoon when Dr. Glasser and Dr. Wazen met with her and informed her that they had gotten the entire tumor out. I was still in the operating room being closed up and would shortly be moved to recovery, and finally the ICU, where I would spend the night. I would be fine.

Her first call was to our parents. Beth had been updating them all day long with progress reports, but this last visit from my doctors was the good news she had been waiting to hear. My Mom later told me that, when she answered the phone, Beth could not even talk, and they simply cried together. Finally, Beth was able to tell our parents that it was over and I was okay. Each word she spoke was broken up with tears of joy. When Mom asked Beth if she were okay, Beth choked out the words "I'm just so emotional." If my wonderful sister had looked in the bag I'd left her, she would have found the box of Kleenex I had provided for her for just this moment.

My very first recollection of waking up from surgery is an interesting one. Remember me telling you about my friend, Diane, whose husband also had had an Acoustic Neuroma? Well, she had told me that her father would be "my OR angel." At the time, I was not quite sure what that meant until she explained, "My dad is a volunteer at Sarasota Memorial and his job is to roll patients from the OR into the recovery area." He happened to be volunteering on the date of my surgery and he would be my angel.

Knowing this, I really wanted to remember him when I came to. And I do recall someone touching my shoulder and saying, "Kathy, wake up! They got the tumor out and you are fine. I want to see your eyes." But when my eyes fluttered open, I was looking at...my Grandpa Miller. Now, you should know that Grandpa Miller and I were really close, and he has been with the Lord for about 20 years.

I shut my eyes again and heard the voice telling me once more to wake up and that I was fine. This time, when I opened my eyes, there was Diane's dad.

Later, Diane would tell me, "You are not going to believe what you said to my dad when you came to!"

I had no recollection of what had happened. Turns out, I used one of the oldest lines in the book: "Did you get the license plate of the Mack truck that hit me?"

Diane's dad laughed and told me that he did not, but he would tell his daughter that I had not lost my sense of humor.

Soon I was moved to the ICU ward to begin the process of recovery. My room was dimly lit with all kinds of colored lights around me that responded to my heart beat, breathing and who knows what else. My bed was positioned so it faced the doorway and I could see the nurses out there. My neck and head were starting to hurt and I really wanted to change position, but I was scared that I might damage some work that had just been done or worse yet, that my brain or brain fluid would leak out, and I would get meningitis.

So, I called out for help, but my voice was not respond-ing the way I wanted it to. I mustered my loudest yell for help and it came out like a pitiful, high-pitched whisper that no one could hear. I tried it twice and got no response. Then I vaguely remembered someone telling me there was a button near my left hand. I felt around and pushed it. Immediately, I heard someone asking me what I needed, and all I could do was respond in that tiny, pip-squeak voice. It makes me laugh to think of it now.

ICU nurses are incredible! To me, they are like boot camp sergeants, and no one gets past them to disturb the patients. Whatever help is needed gets dispensed quickly and efficiently. When I explained to my nurse that my neck and head were hurt-ing locked in one position, she said, "Oh, here you go, let's just turn you around." She took my head in her hands and moved it to the other side. Just like that! Wow! You mean I could have done that? The nurse gave me some ice chips, a shot of some-thing for the pain and I was ready for my night in ICU.

I dozed on and off. At one point I opened my eyes to see my friend Mary walking toward me. Later Mary told me that my ICU nurse said that I was sleeping and informed her, in no uncertain terms, that I was not to be bothered. Mary said, "But her eyes are open! I will not stay long." Mary has had a lot of experience with nurses and hospitals from her own bout with colon cancer and she was anxious to check in on me. Tubes, stitches and hospitals did not frighten her. She came into my room and sat with me for a while, telling me that I looked great and that she heard everything had gone really well. She fed me some ice chips, held the little pan while I threw up and then gave me some more ice chips. What a buddy!

The night passed with a few more calls for help, getting my little pan ready for when I became sick to my stomach and having my vitals checked every hour. I had a CT scan scheduled for 5:30 a.m. on December 31, and I got to a ride down the hall on a gurney. I tried to help the nurses move me, but they insisted I let them do the work. My 5'9" frame took up the length of the gurney, and I remember one of them saying, "She sure is a tall drink of water!"

When the sunlight started to come in the room and announce it was New Years Eve day, it lit up my spirit, too. My nurse suggested I eat something because the nausea was coming and going. She recommended a little applesauce. I had two bites. She had me sit up and actually moved me into a chair in the room, so when my sister and friend LaVerne came in they were happy to see me up and about. One of my doctors checked on me and gave me the go ahead to move out of ICU into a regular room.

In short order I was riding in a wheel chair to my new room on the 9th floor overlooking Sarasota Bay with a view of the Ringling Bridge. I had the room to myself – that is if you don't count all of my friends that came by.

Beth tells me that day one out of surgery went like this: I ate a little, drank, had frosty lip gloss applied, talked with friends that came by, napped, had more frosty lip gloss put on, and so on. I had a couple bites of a saltine cracker for supper, and my sister scolded me, "A mouse would eat more than that!" It was the best I could do at the time. Beth finally slipped out early in the evening and I prepared for my New Years Eve party.

As it turned out, I woke up around 11:45 p.m. on December 31. I put on a 2009 paper tiara and got the noise maker ready! I watched the ball drop on TV, told the nurses on my floor "Happy New Year" and then promptly fell back to sleep with the tiara still on my head.

Even though I celebrated the first day of the New Year in a hospital room – my sister and 30 or more friends came and went that day – apparently I had a blast! While I am told I was very charming and looked great, frankly, I do not remember too much about it thanks to morphine, but I am pleased with the report and grateful that my friends kept the frosty pink lip gloss coming.

Everyone seemed to enjoy the story about how the hole in my head was plugged. You see, once the hole is drilled through the temporal bone, it has to be filled up to keep the brain fluid in and then patched with something my surgeon called "bone paste." I decided not to pursue that part. But the way the hole gets plugged interested me: my surgeons used a fat graft – from my backside. Needless to say, my friends immediately – and lovingly – called me "fat head" and "butt head."

As the medication doses were being lowered and administered less frequently, I was becoming more and more motivated to go home. But first I had to do more walking outside of my room in the hallway. The hospital provided me with an adult sized walker. I'd lean on the front bar and trot around the loop of the 9th floor with my sister in tow, guiding my saline solution and whatever else I was hooked up to at the time. The trot was actually more of a very slow shuffle with occasional stops to make sure I was doing okay and not getting dizzy.

It all seemed to be going great!

I am so grateful to all of my wonderful friends, family and neighbors. They made sure I was comfortable and insisted that

I did not lift a finger during my recovery, taking care of nearly every need I had. I love every one of them dearly.

> *Brothers, I do not consider myself yet to have taken hold of it. But one thing I do: Forgetting what is behind and straining toward what is ahead,*
>
> *Philippians 3:12-13*

Post Op

On Friday, January 2, 2009, I was released from the hospital. I couldn't wait to get outside into the sunshine and wanted to operate the wheelchair I was in myself to hurry things along. After I finally got rolled out the sliding doors, I just kept smiling up at the sky as I waited for my sister to pull my car around, loaded with flowers and gifts, and drive me home. I was craving a Subway turkey sandwich, so she made a quick stop for me. We also picked up a prescription for pain pills before heading to my house in Bradenton. There's no place like home!

The first afternoon was delightful – little naps interspersed with visits from people in my neighborhood, members of my church and other friends. The phone rang often and more flowers arrived. Some people were surprised I was home so soon – after only four days – and called me up to say "Hey! We're at the hospital to see you and you aren't here!"

All things considered, I was feeling pretty good, but an occasional bout of nausea reminded me that I had just had major surgery and needed to take it easy. There was a hole in my head covered with staples that had to be treated with extra care. I was still worried about sneezing and trying to figure out what

I to do when I couldn't stop myself. When it finally happened, I yelled out to my sister, "I just sneezed!" and she yelled back, "God bless you!" All a part of getting back to normal.

When I lay down in my own bed the first night, for some reason I felt tremors. It was such a weird sensation, I thought we were having an earthquake. I remember getting up and slowly making my way to the room where my sister was asleep and waking her up. She groggily inquired, "What are you talking about?" I asked her, "Didn't you feel that? Everything is shaking!" She told me go back to bed and get some rest – and even if we were having an earthquake, she would be able to sleep though it just fine. Later I would ask my neurosurgeon about it, and he could not explain why it had happened. It probably had more to do with my finally relaxing and the remnants of the anesthesia leaving my system.

When it was time for my sister Beth to go home, I was fortunate to have another friend come stay with me. Her name was Cindy and she hailed from Houston, Texas. A working mom in a bustling church office, mother of two adorable little girls, Lilli Ann and Ella Grace, and wife to one of my favorite guys in the whole world, Pastor Brad – she leads a busy life. So taking time off to be with me was a sacrifice, but Cindy had insisted, "No matter what! I will be there."

Cindy arrived on the evening of my first day home from the hospital. Over the next week, she took me to my follow-up doctor's appointments. She made sure I was drinking plenty of water and encouraged me to eat more. My appetite was slowly returning and the feelings of nausea were all but gone now. We went on walks, although they were at a snail's pace and for only a couple blocks or so. We also had some lovely lunches at

Sharky's, an old-Florida restaurant on the beach in Venice, and at the Sand Bar on Anna Maria Island, one of the scenic Gulf keys near my home in Bradenton.

January 6, 2009, one week after my surgery, the staples in my head were removed and my neurosurgeon said I was doing great! Cindy insisted that we treat the occasion like an anniversary and celebrate. So we took champagne flutes and some bubbly and drove the short distance to Anna Maria Island to watch the sun set over the Gulf of Mexico and make a festive toast. With my glass raised to the stunning sunset, I toasted my health, the many, many blesssings in my life and hope for my future. It was a beautiful, cool evening, the sunset was spectacular, and it felt wonderful to be alive. It just blew my mind that only one short week ago, I had been lying in ICU and wondering if my brain fluid would leak out. I was feeling ecstatic – as if my life were overflowing with joy and moving to a new level.

When we got home Cindy suggested I write a prayer to go along with the picture she took of me toasting the sunset – the very picture that is on the cover of this book – and these words flowed from my pen into my journal:

Almighty Heavenly Father,

One week ago today you held me tightly
in the palm of your hand
and protected me during brain surgery.

Today, I stand in awe of your wonder and majesty in this
sunset created by you for me.

I raise my hand with the fruit of the vine
to praise, glorify and honor you.
Thank you for blessing me in so many ways.

I am looking forward to discovering the plans
you have in store for me.

Which I know are to help me prosper
and not do me harm.

Your plan is HOPE for my future!

Thank you, Father – I love you!

To God be the Glory!

In Jesus' precious name,
AMEN

Do not be anxious about anything, but in everything, by prayer and petition, with thanksgiving, present your requests to God.

Philippians 4:6

Prayer

Speaking of prayer, I think that the story of my faith is actually quite ordinary. Faith has always been a part of my life – no blinding light, burning bush or other amazing event ever occurred – and I am very glad about that.

When I moved to Florida in 1981, there were a few years when I chose to stay away from church. I was in my early 20s, and Sundays were my days to sleep in after staying out late Saturday nights with friends. Getting up and going to Bible study was definitely not in the cards. Not that I quit believing in God. It was just that after I moved away from home, my new friends had not experienced the upbringing I had had, and their lives. free of worship services, looked appealing. So I tried it. Plus, I now lived near a beautiful beach which, admittedly, was a great place to spend Sunday mornings.

Prayer, on the other hand, has always been a part of my life, even when I didn't go to church. So many times in my life when I felt like I could not do anything else, I always have known I can pray.

As you know, the story of my trifecta of troubles is woven very tightly with a prayer thread. In fact, I had so many prayer warriors fighting for me, it was actually like a prayer rope!

So, the first thing I did when I decided to reach out to others with the news of my brain tumor was ask for prayer. I have no idea how many prayer lists my name was on. I received about 300 get-well cards and hundreds of e-mails during the time I had the brain surgery and was recovering, and many of them were from people I don't even know, but they had prayed for me. They read on their prayer list or in e-mail messages that a woman in Florida needed to have brain surgery, and they prayed for me.

I believe that there is power in prayer and that the power comes not just from a person, but straight from above.

By the way, after those first few years in Florida when I spent Sunday mornings at the beach or slept in, I finally did find a new church family. I now know that, for me, church works. I feel better when I go and I love the fellowship of my friends.

> *Therefore I tell you, whatever you ask in prayer, believe you have received it, and it will be yours"*
> *Mark 11:24*

Keeping a Journal

Watch your thoughts,
 for they become words.
Watch your words,
 for they become actions.
Watch your actions,
 for they become habits.
Watch your habits,
 for they become character.
Watch your character,
 for it becomes your destiny.

— *Anonymous*

Journaling has been a powerful tool for me to get through the lows and back to the highs. Telling a blank page my story helps put my thoughts in perspective. Journaling has been helpful during tough times, such as the dissolution of my marriage and, of course, in 2008 when I was reeling from the triple blow of extraordinary events. In fact, my journal entries are the longest and most descriptive when I am at a low point. It helps me to write out my thoughts as they come, like a free flowing stream. Words just pour out of the pen and onto the pages.

There were times when my journal reflected so many thoughts and feelings written with such anger I can hardly make out the words. I thought that if I pressed down really hard as I wrote, the words would just carry those angry feelings straight to God and anyone else that would listen.

My journal entry on December 2, 2008 reads, "YOU HAVE GOT TO BE KIDDING ME! A BRAIN TUMOR? WHAT WILL I DO NOW?????? I HAVE NO ONE TO TALK TO ABOUT THIS I AM ALL ALONE AND I AM SUPPOSED TO DEAL WITH THIS ALL NOW? I CAN'T DO IT. I CAN'T DO IT. I CAN'T DO IT. GOD – WHY ME????"

Note that these words were all written in capital letters. In the journal they were about two inches tall! When you use all caps in e-mail, it is supposed to convey that you are yelling. Well, I was yelling at the top of my voice at God when I wrote that entry. The ink of that particular page is also smeared with tears I shed – tears of rage, fear and hurt.

My journal also has the word "WHY" written down a lot. That question never seemed to get answered, at least not right away.

I have no idea how someone deals with tragic news, such as terminal cancer or a child or a spouse dying. I can only imagine that the person must be feeling a thousand times worse than I did, and I am very sorry for what he or she must be experiencing. I can only offer encouragement and hope. Write out your feelings and shout out to God. He will hear your cries. Ask him every day to reveal why this has happened to you, and in time, He will.

If you have never written in a personal journal before, just start somewhere – use the margins of this book or, pick up a spiral notebook and pen, or make a new folder in your computer. It takes only a few minutes to record your thoughts and feelings, and I think you will enjoy this private time for your innermost thoughts. In our busy lives we take such little time to do things just for ourselves. So, treat yourself.

What are you thinking you want to do in the next chapter of your life? What obstacles are you facing right now and what questions do you have? Write it all down and begin your journey. Write down your blessings and worries every day. Record your thoughts and they just may become your destiny.

In the beginning was the Word, and the Word was with God, and the Word was God.

John 1:1

Tell Your Story

As I was healing from brain surgery and facing the unemployment line, it occurred to me that maybe the experiences I went through might be of help to someone else. So, I decided to document my story from the notes in my journals; and that is how this little book began.

In the process of reaching out to others and telling everyone about what had happened to me, I also came into contact with a number of people in similar situations to mine. I have had the opportunity to speak to Acoustic Neuroma Association support groups and talk with many AN patients on the phone and online.

One Friday night at one in the morning, I was chatting online with a woman whose surgery was scheduled for the following Monday.

She asked me, "Why would this have happened?"

I could feel her despair even from a distance coming through the computer, so I wrote her back, "I do not know what this all means for you, and I am so sorry you are facing this. But I now realize why I had a brain tumor – it was to encourage you in this difficult time."

When we get real with people and allow our experiences to offer help and support to others, then those tough times don't have to be wasted. Maybe that is the answer to those one word questions in my journal, "WHY?"

The lesson I leave you with here is this: Tell your story. It may connect with people in ways you never imagined. Nothing in our life is wasted when we allow it to be used for good. I have been surprised how many people have been able to relate to me and my story – a farm girl from Indiana who grew up going to church with no major challenges in her life until recently – and gather hope and inspiration from it.

So make connections with people. Tell your story. I imagine that somewhere along the line, your life experience will be of help and comfort to someone else. If a brain tumor or the closing of a bank or a milestone birthday I wasn't looking forward to somehow resonates with you, it is my wish and prayer that you will feel comfort and hope. Hang in there! If you do, I am certain that you will soon see that you have something to celebrate!

The Spirit of the Sovereign Lord is on me, because the Lord has anointed me to preach good news to the poor. He has sent me to bind up the brokenhearted to proclaim freedom for the captives and release from darkness the prisoners.
Isaiah 61:1

Divine Appointments

I don't believe in coincidences. I don't think that it is an accident that you are reading this book. For some reason it has found its way into your hands as a gift, a purchase or in some other way. I think that the coincidences we experience in our life are often little surprise gifts from God. He is speaking to us through them. I'm with my friend Susan on this one. She calls them "divine appointments." The Lord gave me some precious divine appointments during my experiences in 2008.

Months before the bank closed, my birthday and my Acoustic Neuroma diagnosis, I was asked by a local Christian radio station if I could volunteer at a concert event for the group Selah. I had eagerly agreed because this happens to be one of my favorite singing groups. But when the concert date came around on the Friday night, right after I had received the news about my brain tumor, I almost begged off. Too much had happened! But then something inside me said, "Do it! Do it anyway!"

So, on the night of December 5, I went to the concert to serve as a volunteer. My job was to work in the VIP room: greet the station's high contributors and offer them a beverage and a snack while they waited to meet the Selah artists, Todd, Amy and Alan, an hour or so before the concert and have their photo taken with them. Toward the end of the gathering, right before the concert, the station manager asked me if I would like to meet Selah. Would I! He didn't have to ask twice.

Keep in mind that by then I was telling everyone I met to put me on their prayer lists, so when I was introduced to the Selah singers and they politely asked me, "How are you?," I blurted out the story about my brain tumor, the bank closing at the time of my milestone birthday and my need for prayer! I still wonder what Todd, Amy and Alan must have thought when those words leapt out of my mouth. But you know what? They literally wrapped their arms around me and prayed with me right then and there!

I had selected a seat in a row in the back of the sanctuary of the church where the concert was taking place. I wanted to just sit there and worship and enjoy the music. So, about half an hour into the show, as I was taking delight in the songs and words, I heard Todd between songs telling the crowd of about 700, "We just had the chance to meet a woman named Kathy, and she has a brain tumor. I want to ask everyone to pray for her right now."

Oh my goodness! I could not believe my ears!

And then, on top of it, my favorite group dedicated their next song to me. I had not told them that my very favorite song was "Press On." And, don't you know, that's the very song they sang for me. Coincience? I don't think so.

As I sat in that dark concert hall and listened to the words, I had a vision of the Creator of the Universe. He was leaning over to some angels nearby and looking at the scene below and with a big laugh said, "Watch this! She thought she was coming to serve tonight – but I have a special gift just for her!" I can hardly write these words without getting chill bumps. And to think I almost missed out on that divine appointment when I thought of skipping the event. I am so glad that I said to the radio station, "Yes, of course I can still volunteer."

After I had recovered from my brain surgery and was getting back to a regular life routine, I spent time on Facebook reconnecting with people all over the country. I found one friend named Wendy. We had not talked with each other for some time. When I filled her in about my job loss and the brain tumor, she immediately wrote back, "You have got to meet my friend Ellen Menard!" Wendy said we had a lot of things in common, including the fact that we both lived in the Sarasota-Bradenton area.

It turns out that Ellen was also a brain surgery patient with an Acoustic Neuroma! She checked into Sarasota Memorial Hospital on the day I checked out. Like me, Ellen was also a human resources executive, and she had just finished her first book, *The Not So Patient Advocate*, a helpful resource guide for anyone facing a medical crisis. You may not be dealing with a major illness right now, but chances are that you or someone you know will down the road, and this book will tell you how to partner with your health care providers for successful outcomes.

A few weeks after we made contact, Ellen and I finally met at a coffee shop for what I thought would be an hour or so. After nearly two hours of non-stop talking about our parallel lives, we had bonded.

It was my meeting with Ellen and finding out about *The Not So Patient Advocate* that gave me the confidence to go forward with my own book. Coincidence? I don't think so.

I am convinced that my meeting Ellen was a divine appointment through Wendy. I just have a feeling that our friendship will continue to grow and that we both can help each other in ways we never imagined. I know there are wonderful things in store for both of us. Think about your last few days. What has been going on with you? Why you might have a divine appointment reading this book right now, at this time of your life, in whatever circumstance you are facing. There is a reason we are meeting here between these pages.

In the meantime, may God bless you with more lovely surprises and miracles today.

> *If you have a message of encouragement for the people, please speak.*
> *Acts 13: 15*

Highs and Lows

Speaking of divine appointments, my next door neighbors are the Breeden family – Janet, Bob and their daughter Claire. I love them like my own family. As a single person with no children, it is especially nice to have such a lovely group of people next door. They fill a void in so many ways and I am forever grateful for the close friendship we have shared during the last four years since I moved in next door to them.

There are many special things about the Breedens. Janet is a brilliant, caring and well-organized wife, mother and pediatrician. Plus, she makes the best grilled hamburgers I have ever had, and I thank her for sharing her secret recipe with me.

Janet knew that I would not be able to drive after my surgery, so she offered to pick up my friend Cindy when she flew in from Texas for the second shift of my care. Since Beth did not know the route to the Tampa airport and I could not drive, Janet insisted on making the hour-long trip to pick up Cindy for me. Janet is thoughtful and caring like that.

Bob, is a great husband, father, cook and musician. He has helped me when I needed furniture moved and once he even offered to get a dead rat out of my attic. Fortunately for Bob, my pest control company showed up in time to retrieve the rodent before he had to. But you know what? He would have done it! Bob is thoughtful and caring like that.

Claire is one of my favorite people in the whole wide world. Eleven-years-old, she is not only adorable, but also witty and brilliant: She is just plain fun to be around. When I came home from the hospital, Claire "babysat" me the evening her mother drove Cindy back to the airport. This was my first time alone, so it was nice of Claire to "watch me." She made a great nurse! Claire and I can have fun together sitting, reading, drawing or playing a game. I hope that everyone gets to have a Claire in their life.

Take care of the little angels in your life. Share some time with them and enjoy their company. If they are anything like my Claire, they will make you laugh a lot and probably teach you many amazing lessons. I just know that I will go to Claire's wedding one day, and she will be at my funeral with a whole lot of fun times in between.

It was the Breeden family who taught me the "High and Low" game. They reminded me that while there are some not-so-good things in your life, there are always good things that happen to everyone every day.

Here is how the game works: After dinner everyone at the table tells the group what his or her High and Low was for the day. It is interesting because no matter how low your lowest day might be, there is always something to smile about and celebrate. One time, Bob's High and Low were the same thing. He had been working a job that took him out of town away from Janet and Claire all week. It was great that the job ended so he could be at home with his family, but it was also a Low because the job had ended. And sometimes life is just like that: bittersweet.

For me, it was a definite Low to find out I had a brain tumor, but it became an amazing High because of all of the things that happened as a result. I have reconnected with people, had the chance to share my story, write this book and, ultimately, come to a whole new relationship with God. A brand new High level!

It is okay to have the sad moments that form your Lows. Take them to the Lord. Cry on His shoulder, crawl up in His lap and let Him know the desires of your heart. It will not be too long before He pulls you up to a High you could never have imagined! God is so good. All of the time! It says in the book of Psalms to "Delight yourself in the Lord and he will give you the desires of your heart."

God just cracks me up sometimes. He blessed me with the bank closing to give me the time to write a book. It was a Low for the bank to close at the same time of my 50th birthday, but it has been a High to tell my story. Had it not been for the brain tumor, unemployment and milestone birthday, I really do not think I would have taken the opportunity to use my testimony to deliver a message of hope to others. I have had the chance to speak to many groups and offer an encouraging message. Reporters have interviewed me and put my picture and story on the cover of newspapers, and a neighbor recently came by to say "thank you" for sharing my story because it touched many people at his office.

I am delighted in God and have discovered that in the highs and the lows he will always take good care of me. Go ahead and try it! Delight yourself in Him and see if He does not give you the desire of your heart. And by the way, do not forget to be thankful for your Lows, because it is *very* possible they may turn into an amazing new High one day.

> *Delight yourself in the Lord and he will give you the desires of your heart.*
>
> **Psalm 37:4**

A Grateful Heart

It is so easy to say thank you when everything in your life is going along fine. But I believe that the Creator of the Universe must be especially pleased with his children when they say thank you for the tough times.

Saying thank you for a tumor was not easy, but I did it, and I have been blessed indeed. My experiences in 2008 have brought my relationship with God to a new level. I know that I have been called by God to share this message of hope and encouragement.

Gratitude is a good feeling to have. Giving thanks in all circumstances is not easy but I can attest to the fact that when you do that, your heart will start changing and your outlook will begin to improve. Not all at once and not necessarily very fast, but little by little.

After I had my surgery I took the opportunity to write the Acoustic Neuroma Association (ANA) a thank you letter. When I was first diagnosed with my tumor, the ANA sent me and my parents a lot of useful information. As a result of my thank you note, I was asked to write an article for their quarterly newsletter, which appeared in June of 2009. I have since received many e-mails and messages from people all over the country.

Some had already had surgery to remove, or partially remove, their Acoustic Neuroma. Others were about to have surgery and needed to talk to someone.

Even though I said, "Thank You" to God shortly after I received the diagnosis about my brain tumor, it took a long time before I could say it with all my heart. It took even longer for me to be grateful. I think God must have trusted me a great deal to give me the task to take my problems of unemployment, my milestone birthday and a brain tumor to a level of gratitude.

As a result, my faith in God has been elevated to a new height. Today I can express my gratitude for that trust placed in me. And I can only urge you to give thanks whenever you can – on good occasions and in times of trouble. The rewards will be manifold.

When I have the chance to speak to groups I always reference the scripture from I Thessalonians that says: "Be Joyful Always. Pray Continually. Give thanks in all circumstances." Saying thank you for the good stuff in our life is easy. But I have found that when I am grateful for the tough times, I open myself up to eventually receiving an extra sense of peace that comes from some of those divine appointments I mentioned as well as an inner calm. You can gain a new strength in your mind and your soul and just like any fitness or diet regime for the body, practicing a constant attitude of gratitude will have its rewards.

> *Be cheerful no matter what; pray all the time; thank God no matter what happens. This is the way God wants you who belong to Christ Jesus to live.*
> *1 Thessalonians 5:16-17*

Afterword

Since the writing of this book, I have found a job in Jacksonville, Florida, with, of all things, the FDIC. It is a temporary assignment, and I come home on many weekends. I've been told the job will end after two years, and who knows what will happen after that.

But somehow, the worries of unemployment, insurance and health do not really matter the way they used to. I am safely nestled in the palm of the Master's hand. What better place to be! I know that the Creator of the Universe has a payroll budget that will meet all of my needs, an insurance plan that will always protect me and the very best retirement plan of all!

These days I am feeling great. Although I have completely lost hearing in my left ear, I still have a good ear on the other side. To compensate I have taught myself some basic sign language. Remember the song "Press On"? I often end my speaking engagements now by "singing" it in sign language while Selah provides the vocals from a CD.

In the meantime, I am getting ready to start training for the 2010 Indianapolis Half Marathon with my sister and friends. Once again, my birthday was celebrated with the FDIC, at my new job, but this time it was fun. What a difference a year makes!

I now prepare for the next extraordinary event in my life, and I promise you I intend to meet it just as I did the tumor, the bank failure and my milestone birthday – with the support of friends, with the peace of God and with a grateful heart, whatever the circumstance. I am confident I will be just fine.

Kahil Gibran, a Lebanese-born American novelist and essayist, wrote, "We choose our joys and sorrows long before we experience them." The choice we make about a particular event in our life may impact just our future or include the lives of others down the road. We mold and create the consequences of our life by the choices we make every day. If Gibran is right, then what choices did you make yesterday, last week or last year? Are they reflecting joy or sorrow today?

Consider the choices you made today, yesterday, last week. How did they work out for you? Knowing what you know now, would you change the way that you reacted? Reflection is an amazing teaching opportunity. Reflect and learn! And as you do all this, have fun with it. You, too, have been blessed with an amazing and unique set of circumstances. Allow those events to propel you to a new and higher level of life. There is a lot to experience and much to learn.

Be grateful for the days ahead and look for those divine appointments.

And whatever challenges you are facing, celebrate them.

So let's get your party started!

I will bring the lip gloss.

Rejoice in the Lord always. And again I say: Rejoice!
Philippians 4:4

Acknowledgment

There are so many people that encouraged me during my trifecta of extraordinary events in 2008 that there isn't room enough to thank them all here. They were there for me with lots of support through talks and prayers and love. I would like to especially thank:

My parents, Betty & Charlie Mattick.

My sisters, Beth Dailey and Charlene Seidner.

My brothers-in-law and niece, Mark Dailey, Chris Seidner and Chelsea Linville.

My church family at First Baptist Church in Sarasota, Florida.

My Leadership Manatee Group in Bradenton, Florida and the Manatee Chamber of Commerce and my Eckerd College alums.

My co-workers and friends at the former Freedom Bank in Bradenton, Florida.

All of the friends I have made through the Florida Banker's Association, especially Pete Brokaw, Alex Sanchez and Yvette Downes and every student and instructor at the Supervisor's Academy in Orlando.

My neighbors at the Inlets in Manatee County and my neighbors on Longboat Key.

Tobi & Gaspare Martino, Pam and Nelson Fox, Scott Coulter, Julie Herrmann, Carmen Danner, Jeff Turner, Jo & Dennis Keating, Kathy Connelly, Jen Robinson, Tammy Kiehl, Cindy Benedict, Stacy Byers, Dan and Janet Cracchiola, Eric and Julie Want, Pastor Bill and Beverly Hild, Tina Purcell, Dr. Jim and Nancy Brandenburg, LaVerne & Paul Maus, Gerry & Lisa Anthony, Cindy, Brad, Ella and Lilli Heintz, the entire Mattick family, the entire Miller family, Donna Hardesty and her special family, Judy Buress, Pam & Sarah Gilley, Kathy & Keith Christie, Marilyn & Jim Buchholz, Dr. Burt Bertram, Mary Colonese, Doug & Jamie Badertscher.

My funk sisters: Mary Pierson, Diney Minks and Melody Kelly. Jody & Lisa Hudgins, Mouse Hearin, Linda Potts, Dave and Shirley Duncan, Nick Zec, Kim Reed, Roxanne Rosell & Bob Moravec, Darlene & Rick Kunkel, Sandy, Rick & Irina La-Rose and all the lovely ladies at the Design 2000 salon, Mason Rogers & the 2008 Fall Boot Camp Class at Lifestyle Family Fitness and all of the trainers at LFF.

Diane Muir, George Tatge, Ellen & Arthur Menard, Lesley Coble, Chuck Wilson, David Zuern, Frank Knautz, Jim Teague, Anna Lufi, Dr. Jack Wazen, Dr. Ryan Glasser, Dr. Mark Van Ess, Debbie Graber, Lacie McPeek, Julie Daugherty, Dr. Jack Thompson, Patti, Barbara and David Donnelly, Rick & Debbie Howell, Cherri Leetzow, Mary Binswanger, Arthur Cook, Frank Norris, Debra Harrell, Amy Anderson, Maggie Thompson, Rich "Rico" Hull, Maribeth Leaman, Claire, Janet & Bob Breeden, Bill Geary, Skip & Beth Martin, Charlie & Andrea Bailey, Kristen & Taylor Sweeney, Tonya Maxey (you were my confirmation!).

Everyone at The Parable Living Word Bookstore, Michael Gayon and the Alpha & Omega Café, Selah, all my friends at

Life 89.1, the wonderful professionals at the Silverstein Institute, and the Neurosurgery and Spine Specialists and Sarasota Memorial Hospital.

My Mother saw to it that I was on a lot of prayer lists and some of those church families in Indiana who lifted me up in prayer were: Union Christian Church in Terre Haute, Northside Christian Church in Terre Haute, Mecca New Life Wesleyan in Mecca, Forest Park Baptist in Terre Haute, North Terre Haute Christian Church, Cross Lane Community Church in Terre Haute, Maplewood Christian Church in Terre Haute, Rosedale Baptist Church in Rosedale, Cross Tabernacle in Terre Haute, New Covenant Fellowship Church in Terre Haute, and North Terre Haute Baptist Church. Thank you.

Finally, a huge thank you to my friend, editor and publisher, Chris Angermann. He gave me much encouragement and help.

I always thank God for you! The grace of our Lord Jesus be with you. My love to all of you!
1 Corinthians 1:4 and 16:23-24

A portion of the proceeds of the sale of this book will go to:

The Acoustic Neuroma Association
600 Peachtree Pkwy, Suite 108
Cumming, GA 30041-6899
Phone: (770) 205-8211 or 1-877-200-8211
www.anausa.org

Samaritan Counseling Services of the Gulf Coast
3224 Bee Ridge Road
Sarasota, Florida 34239
Phone (941) 926-2959
www.samaritangulfcoast.com

Ear Research Foundation
1901 Floyd St
Sarasota, Florida 34239
(941) 366-9222
www.earsinus.com

If you wish to contact Katherine Robinson directly, you
can reach her at her websites:

www.expectthebest.org